Prophetic Session

Your Workbook Manual for Adolescents and Young Adults

For Volume 100 & 101

Ashley Reynolds

Prophetic Session: Your Workbook Manual for Adolescent and Young Adults

For Volume 100 & 101

By: Ashley Reynolds

Book Cover: Jasmine Miller

Published by J. Elaine Writes

www.jelainewrites.com

This document is published by J. Elaine Writes located in the United States of America. It is protected by the United States Copyright Act, all applicable state laws and international copyright laws.

Printed in the United States of America

ISBN: 978-1-7332352-5-9

Manual Dedication

This Manual is dedicated to all of the youth and young adults who feel as though the Lord has called them into the ministry of the prophet. It is my earnest prayer that you take these basic principles and apply them to your young prophetic lives. I can assure you that if you utilize these books and manual along with the bible and other prophetic book materials, you will grow integrally at an accelerated rate.

Recorded Prophets of the Bible:

The Prophets (Men)

Jesus (Chief Prophet)

Abraham

Isaac

Jacob

Moses

Aaron

Joshua

Phineas

Samuel

Gad

Nathan

David

Iddo

Michaiah son of Imlah

Obadiah

Ahijah the Shilonite

Jehu son of Hanani

Azariah son of Oded

Jahaziel the Levite

Eliezer son of Dodavahu

Hosea

Amos

Micah

Amoz

Elijah

Elisha

Jonah son of Amittai

Isaiah

Joel

Nahum

Habakkuk

Zephaniah

Uriah

Jeremiah

Ezekiel

Shemaiah

Baruch

Neriah

Seraiah

Mehseiah

Haggai

Zechariah

Malachi

Mordecai Bilshan

Oded

Hanani

The Prophetesses (Women)

Miriam

Deborah

Hannah

Abigail

Huldah

Esther

Prophetic Manual Table of Contents:

The Prophet of God

"And He Himself gave some to be apostles, some prophets, some evangelists, and some pastors and teachers." - Ephesians 4:11 (NKJV)

"The Prophet is Gods choice."- Ashley Reynolds

1. What is a prophet? According to Exodus 4:15-16, it reveals 3 things about what a prophet is:

    a. the prophet is as God to the people- "16b" (CSB) "you will serve as God to him." - I am in no way saying that you are "God" most high, but according to this verse and Psalms 82:6- "I said, 'You are "gods"; you are all sons of the Most High.'"; you have God's permission to "act" as him on the earth. So, now you will have to study how God acts. You will need to know what his character and integrity is, so that you can mimic it among people.

        i. God reigns on his throne as God. We always say if God does not do anything else, he is still God. This means that the being of God is not tied to works. This also means that God is still who he is even if he chooses not to do what he does (function as God; healing, blessings, protection, etc). Well if God told Moses that he would be as God to the people, this meant that Moses, the prophet, would not be a prophet on the basis of prophetic function (speaking), but whether on the truth that God called him to be one. Am I eliminating the prophet's ability to speak? Absolutely not. However, what I am saying is that a prophet is not a prophet because he speaks, but because God elected him to be one.

    b. The prophet is one who discerns the mind and will of God- "15a", "You will speak with him and tell him what to say."- we can see that God chooses to reveal to Moses what's on His heart and mind.

    c. Has the ability to speak and do works for God. Exodus "15b", "I will help both you and him to speak and will teach you both what to do."

2. Who calls the prophet?

        a. Deuteronomy 18:15 (NKJV)

        b. Jeremiah 1:5 (NKJV)

3. Where are prophets usually found? God chooses His prophets and they are typically found among the common people.

        a. Amos 7: 15 NKJV

        b. Deuteronomy 18:15 NKJV

4. What is the job of the prophet?? Let's examine what was said of the prophet John by the angel of the Lord according to Luke 1:16-17 (GNT). Let's look at a few truths of what the prophet does:

      a. A prophet goes before the Lord in a powerfully strong prophetic spirit

      b. He is reconciliation for broken relationships

      c. A prophet has the ability to turn people back to righteousness by correcting wayward thinking

      d. He prepares people for the arrival of Christ

      e. He also is a spokesman for God to people (Jeremiah 1:7) (Deuteronomy 18:18)

5. What are some common hesitancies or reactions of the chosen prophet? Let's examine some Scriptures NKJV

      a. Exodus 4:10- speech inadequacy

      b. Jeremiah 1:6- fear for lack of words

      c. Jeremiah 1:8-Afraid

      d. Jeremiah 1 :17- Dismay

      e. Jonah 1:1-3- Flee/run

6. What should prophets avoid?

      a. Luke 1:15-NKJV wine or hard liquor

      b. Deuteronomy 18:20- NKJV

            i. Speaking presumptuously in the name of God

            ii. Speaking in the name of other "gods"

7. How do we know when a prophet speaks presumptuously?

      a. Deuteronomy 18:22-NKJV when a word spoken in the Lord's name does not manifest

      b. What is on the line when someone says, "the Lord said and the thing said does not come to pass?"

            i. The Lord's name

            ii. The integrity of the prophetic mantle

            iii. The belief or trust of the people in this chosen ministry

8. How does God see a prophet that He chooses?

    a. Luke 1:15NKJV- God sees his prophets as being great

       i. This is encouragement for the prophet to know that he/she is great in the sight of the Lord even when people do not see them as being relevant or significant.

9. Prophets are called to _____ in the _____ _____ of God. As a result, it will cause God's people to _____ his _____. (Jeremiah 23:22 NKJV)

10. Young prophet, if God does not _____ you, then you do not _____. If God has not _____ to you, then do not _____. (Jeremiah 23:21) NKJV

11.) What is the motive of a false prophet?

    a. Read Jeremiah 23: 25-27; you will find your answer in verses 26b; 27 NKJV

    b. Read 2 Peter 2: 1-3 (NIV)

12.) What is the typical behavior of false prophets? Scripture reference: Jeremiah 23:13 (NKJV)

    a. They cause God's people to _____.

    b. They also do three things:

       i. Commit adultery

       ii. Walk in lies

       iii. Strengthen the hands of the evil doers

13. Note that according to 1 Corinthians 14:32, how prophets have prophetic spirits given by God which works hand in hand with the Holy Spirit. They are born with a prophetic nature. The job of the Holy Spirit is to assist with sharpening and directing what their prophetic mantles should be while in the earth.

We hope that you have learned something from this lesson

*This is the end of this section. *

What is Prophecy?

"Pursue love, and desire spiritual gifts but especially that you may prophesy."
- 1 Corinthians 14:1(NKJV)
"Prophesy prophet. prophesy until you see in the earth what you saw in the spirit." - Ashley Reynolds

1. According to Dr. Paula Price, prophecy can be broken up and defined as: pro "beforehand" or "time" and phemi "saying". So, in essence, prophecy is a word or saying before time. This means that the prophet has the ability to speak a word before its time and season to manifest. This is the confusing part for many, because the present day circumstances will not favor the word spoken. However, people must be careful not to discount the word spoken out of the mouth of the prophet.

2. According to Genesis 18:17 (NKJV), it teaches that:

        a. God does not hide his plan from his prophets (Amos 3:7- is a reference point for this)

        b. Prophecy is the mind of God

        c. It is the hidden will of Gods agenda revealed

3. Where does prophecy originate from?

        a. Let's examine 2 Peter 1:20-21 (Living Bible)

            i. For no _____ recorded in Scripture was ever thought up by the _____himself. It was the _____ _____ within these godly men who gave them true _____ from _____.

            ii. So we can see through Scripture that true prophecy begins with God.

4. What is the purpose of prophecy? 1 Corinthians 14:3 (NKJV) lists 3 reasons for prophecy. What are they?

        a.

        b.

        c.

5. To whom is prophecy given for?

1 Corinthians 14:22 (NKJV): therefore _____ are for a sign not to those who_____ but to _____; but _____ is not for _____ but for those who_____.

6. According to 1 Corinthians 14:24-25 (Living Bible) can an unbeliever be positively affected by prophecy? Though prophecy is not for the unbeliever it can impact the lives of the believer in many ways: (vs 24) But if you prophesy, preaching God's word, (even though such preaching is mostly for believers) and the _____ _____ or a _____ _____ comes in who does not understand about these things, all these _____ will _____ him of the fact that he is a _____, and his _____ will be pricked by everything he _____. (vs 25) As he _____, his _____ _____ will be laid bare and he will _____ _____ on his knees and _____ _____, declaring that _____ is really _____ you.

7. Should we put all of our confidence in prophecy? Let's examine the story of Hezekiah in 2 Kings

_____

_____

_____

_____

_____

8. According to 1 Corinthians 13:8 (NKJV), can prophecy fail?

Love never fails, but where there are _____, they will _____. This is why we do not put all of our confidence in prophecy but whether the God of the prophecy.

9. 1 Thessalonians 5:20 (NKJV) states that we should not _____; _____.

    a. What do you think the Apostle Paul meant when he said these words?

10. What does prophecy do and to whom does it do it for?

According to 1 Corinthians 14:4 (NKJV): He who speaks in a tongue edifies himself, but he who prophesies _____ (what) the _____ (who)

11. Who can prophesy? Read 1 Corinthians 14:5 (NKJV)_____

_____

_____

_____

12. Should prophecy be judged? Explain your answer. Read 1 Corinthians 14:29 (NKJV)

_____

_____

_____

_____

13. According to 1 Corinthians 14:31 (NKJV), it says that prophecy is orderly and should be released one by one so that everyone will be _____ and _____

14. According to 1 Corinthians 14:39, the Apostle Paul encourages us on how we should be eager to do what? _____ .

We hope that you have learned something from this lesson

*This is the end of this section. *

The Prophet and God Relationship

"The Lord used a prophet to bring Israel up from Egypt, by a prophet he cared for him."
- Hosea 12:13 (NIV)
"Whenever God chose a prophet it was because he had people on His mind."- Ashley Reynolds

1. The relationship between God and his prophets are unique. They have an understanding with one another in such a way that they know each other's thoughts. For the prophet, God is the safe haven that he can confide in to release his innermost being. This is the part of him that most will never come to know. For God, whenever he has a secret that he wants to reveal he will confide in his prophets. Know that God and his prophets have a different kind of dialogue than any other ministry gift except the Apostle. God does not reveal his secrets with everyone. the only people that get the secrets of the Lord are:

      a. His prophets, (Amos 3:7)

      b. Those that truly fear Him. (Psalms 25:14) NASB

2. God will ensure to you how that you are the apple of his eye:

      a. Zechariah (2:8)

3. The prophet is so valuable to God that he will rise to the defense of the prophet:

      a. Genesis 12: 17-20

      b. Numbers 12:1-10 (NIV) (God defends Moses against Miriam and Aaron)

4. God will speak to the prophet ahead of the timing of a prophetic manifestation.

      a. 1 Samuel 9:15

5. Before anything is permitted to happen on earth, the Lord will first have counsel with his prophets.

      a. Amos 3:7; Ezekiel 3:22

6. It is because the prophet loves God that he will stay positioned in the kingdom of God to build Gods house. As a result, the sinner will be both convicted by his sins as well as convinced that God is among you. (1 Corinthians 14: 24-25)

      a. This will make room for God to be known and for souls to realize how God operates through his prophets and thereby souls won to the Lord.

      b. The prophet's main agenda is making Christs name exalted

7. The prophet loves God so much that he wants to look like God in order that he might represent him well in every season of his life.

8. With the God/prophet relationship, God will reassure the prophet on how he wants to use him as his prophet on the earth. This will serve to help keep the prophet true to the prophetic sphere and authority given him. This will also help the prophet to not feel pressured with following other people's prophetic ministry when God has not ordained it to be. It will also keep you from following some of the myths out there about how prophets should operate. The gift is yours but always remember that the operation of your gift belongs to God.

We hope that you have learned something from this lesson

*This is the end of this section. *

Holy Spirit and Prophet Relationship

"above all, you must understand that no prophecy of scripture came about by the prophet's own interpretation. For prophecy never had its origin in the will of man, but men spoke from God as they were carried along by the Holy Spirit." - 2 Peter 1:20-21 (NIV)

"The Holy Spirit is the Wind beneath the Prophets Ministry."- Ashley Reynolds

1. Though prophets are born with a prophetic spirit they still need the assistance of the Holy Spirit for the empowerment and direction of his prophetic mantle. (2 Peter 1:21)

2. The Holy Spirit brings confirmation to the ministry of the prophet- Jesus is the chief Prophet. After John the Baptist baptized Jesus, the spirit of God descended upon him like a dove. (Luke 3 :22)

3. According to the lesson, "Holy Spirit and Prophet Relationship," who promised the Holy Spirit and what was its purpose? (look at Acts 1:4;8)

_____

_____

_____

4. According to the lesson, "Holy Spirit and Prophet Relationship," what is the Hebrew term for Holy   Spirit?

_____

_____

5. According to Acts 1:4, the Holy Spirit would be given on 2 accounts. What were they?

1.

2.

6. Ezekiel 2:2, "the _____ entered me when He (the Lord) _____ to me, and set me on my _____; and I _____ him who _____ to me."

7. According to the lesson, "Holy Spirit and Prophet Relationship," the Holy Spirit is also referred to as the _____ which helps to carry you into your assignment.

We hope that you have learned something from this lesson

*This is the end of this section. *

The Prophet and Mentor Relationship

"Elisha then left his oxen and ran after Elijah..." 1 Kings 19:20 (NKJV)

"Sufficient as water is to life, so the mentor is to the mentee." - Ashley Reynolds

1. What is the role of a mentor?

    a. A mentor brings one under the rod of his mantle (jurisdiction; leadership) for the purposes of teaching and instructing.

        i. The mentor is always one step ahead of the mentee. God allows for the mentor to encounter certain things before he sends him students to teach.

        a. Please note that the people that mentor's mentor are all on different levels:

            i. Some you will have to start from scratch

            ii. Some will only need a little molding

            iii. Mentors mentor people that typically have the same abilities as they do (both Elijah and Elisha were prophets and they were both called to operate in miracles, signs and wonders.)

2. How does the mentor know who he is called to mentor?

    a. God will reveal it to him- 1 Kings 19:16

3. When God reveals who the mentor should mentor, what should the mentor do?

    a. Go after the one he is anointed to mold and shape spiritually- 1 Kings 19: 19

    b. Release his cloak upon the mentee- 1 kings 19:19b

4. What is the purpose of mentorship?

    a. To pray for the mentee - John 17:9

    b. Raises them up- john- 6:39

    c. Provides wise counsel for the mentee's future

5. What should a mentor have for their mentee/s?

    a. A _____ of who the mentee is- Matthew 16:18-19; 1 Kings 19: 17

6. What should the mentor be able to do for the mentee?

    a. _____ _____ - Read Matt 10:1

7. What should the relationship between the mentor and the mentee look like?

    a. Both the mentee and the mentor should have _____ about each by the _____ of _____ - Read Matt 16:16-20

8. When being mentored by your mentor what should you be doing according to proverbs 19:20? (NKJV):

    a. _____ to counsel and _____ instructions. This will be so to ensure that you may be _____ in your _____ days.

    b. So, we see through Proverbs 19:20 (NKJV) that though wise counsel from your mentor can benefit you now, its ultimate purpose is to prepare you for you for your future destiny.

9. We have studied how that the prophecy spoken is both the ____will_____ and the _____mind___ of God.

According to my understanding it is the job of the mentor to instruct the budding prophet that though:

    a. There are many _____ in a _____ heart, nevertheless the _____'s _____ will _____ - Read Proverbs 19:21 (NKJV)

    b. This scripture shows how that the mentor should bring to the mentee's mind that they should always cling to God's counsel, because though he has plans it is only the plan of the Lord that will prevail.

10. Let's look at another responsibility of the mentee found in proverbs 20:5 (NKJV)

    a. _____ in the _____ of man is like_____; but a _____ of _____ will _____ it out.

    b. This scripture shows the mentee that he/she must reach or seek for the information needed to grow. It is a matter of how bad do you want it.

11. Can the mentee teach the mentor? Is God calling you to mentor your mentor?

    a. Through personal experience I have never been in a position whereby I felt led by the Lord to teach my mentors. I have always thought that God was calling me to come under their tutelage to glean their dainties or tree of substance.

    b. Let's read these scriptures: (Jesus/ disciples); Moses/ Joshua, Samuel/Saul- all of these scriptures' points to the truth that it was the mentor that taught and the mentee that receives.

    c. However, though God is not calling the mentee to train the leader; the mentee can minister to the mentor. This can happen in several ways (read:

        i. Seed of prayer for the mentor

ii. support of your mentors' vision

iii. sowing a seed of money into the future of your mentor

iv. being open to receive their substance

Let's examine some situations on when the mentor reaches out to the mentee and when the mentee reaches out to the mentor:

1. Mentee reaches out to the mentor:

a. 1 Kings 19:20-21 (NKJV)

b. 1 Samuel 9:18-22 (NKJV)

2. Mentor reaches out to the mentee:

a. 1 Kings 19:15-16 (NKJV)

b. 1 Samuel 9: 15-17 (NKJV)

c. 1 Samuel 10: 1-10 (NKJV)

We can see through these scriptures on how that the Mentor and Mentee relationship is a partnership. They can strengthen one another. This is the way it should be.

We hope that you have learned something from this lesson

*This is the end of this section. *

The Prophet and Prayer; Why should you Pray?

" Pray Without Ceasing." - 1 Thessalonians 5:17, (NKJV)

"Prayer lights the soul as fire does a candle. The prophet is activated through prayer." - Ashley Reynolds

1. In the Lesson, "The prophet and Prayer; Why should you Pray?," we learned that for the prophet, prayer is _____ and not _____.

2. In the lesson, "The prophet and Prayer; why should you pray", we learned that prophecy is _____ and not _____.

3. According to the lesson, "The prophet and Prayer; why should you pray", we learned six facts about prayer. What are they and explain them:

    1. _____
       _____
       _____
       _____

    2. _____
       _____
       _____
       _____

    3. _____
       _____
       _____
       _____

    4. _____
       _____
       _____
       _____

    5. _____
       _____
       _____
       _____

    6. _____
       _____
       _____
       _____

4. According to the lesson, "The prophet and Prayer; why should you pray", we learned three facts about what prayer is **NOT.** What are they and explain them:

1. _____
_____
_____
_____
_____

2. _____
_____
_____
_____
_____

3. _____
_____
_____
_____
_____

5. Prophets are typically drawn to prayer after they hear a word from the Lord. It is almost as if hearing from the Lord activates a greater desire for the prophet to pray. Let's look at Genesis 12:7 (NKJV) "Then the _____ appeared to _____ and said, "to your descendants _____ will give this land. And there _____ _____ an _____ to the _____, who had _____ to him."

6. In Genesis 12:7, we can also see how when God reveals, he at times reveals a portion of what he intends for the prophet to know. This is used as bait to lure the prophet into his secret chambers by setting aside time to intentionally seek his face.

7. Prayer also has the ability to encourage one to move, "And he _____ from there to the mountain east of _____, and he pitched his tent with _____ on the _____ and Ai on the _____, there he _____ an _____ to the Lord." (Read Genesis 12:8-NKJV)

8. We can see how in Genesis 12:8 that prayer caused Abram to get up and move. This prayer also granted a greater sense of direction to Abram by securing him with knowing that he was on the right path. " so _____ journeyed, going on _____ toward the _____." (Read Genesis 12:9-NKJV)

9. Oftentimes when prophets embark upon their prophetic journeys, they seek for signs that will ensure them that they are on the correct pathway towards destiny. The most reliable thing to depend on to ensure such certainty is prayer or communication with God. We can see that in Genesis 12:9-NKJV, how that Abram ``still'' went on towards his way. This was because he had

gotten alone with God on his altar in order to hear a word from the Lord concerning the direction he had taken.

We hope that you have learned something from this lesson

*This is the end of this section. *

The Prophetic Mind

"Don't be selfish; don't try to impress others. Be humble, thinking of others as better than yourselves"- Philippians 2: 3 (NLT)

"A prophets mind is the gateway for which the agenda of God can flow." - Ashley Reynolds

1. Jesus Christ, son of the living God, was considered as a prophetic manifestation. He came to fulfill all that the prophets had spoken. However, it is my belief that he was our chief prophet. It is through the life of Christ that we can examine what having a prophetic mind was really about. With saying this we should follow the Apostle Paul's instruction found in Philippians 2:5:

"Let this _____ be in _____ which was also in _____ _____."

This simple statement is few in words, yet it is the key that will propel you into exaltation from God.

2. Let's examine in Philippians 2:6-8, how having the mind of Christ will move you over into exaltation from God:

      1. Becoming one of no reputation

      2. Taking on the spirit of a bondservant

      3. Humbling yourself

      4. Becoming obedient to difficult Godly tasks (death on the cross)

3. Through reading Philippians 2:5-8, we can see how having this Christ- like mentality is all about submission to God and to man. We must also know that the mind of Christ is spiritual bound and not carnal.

4. Because the mind of the Prophet is not carnal, but is spiritual let's examine a little on how the prophet Abram was able to obtain and access the will of God:

    Abram:

        a. Humility: What did Abram do when he lifted his eyes and saw the three men standing by him?

        _____

        _____, (Genesis 18:2)

        b. Bondservant: In what ways did Abram serve the three men when they showed up?

        _____

        _____

_____

_____

_____. (Genesis 18:4-8)

5. We should understand as prophetic people that our humble spirit carries the ability to lead us into God's futuristic thoughts concerning our lives. Let's look at how Abrams' mindset of humility and will to become a bondservant to the three men (which one was the Lord) caused the will of the Lord to be revealed to both he and Sarah. Read Genesis 18:9-10, and record what secret was revealed:

_____

_____

_____.

6. In the presence of the Lord you have no reputation. When God shows up it's all about Him and His heavenly agenda. Many people stand in the way of God's agenda because they think that they are important. However, when the prophet relinquishes all rights before the Lord, he will make way for God to prophetically reveal his mind and plan to him. Read (Genesis 18:16-19)

7. The true purpose of this section was to herald the sound of this truth that when you have a prophetic mind it moves you into prophetic dialogue with God for the purpose of having that which was previously hidden brought into your now. (Read Genesis 18:20-32)

We hope that you have learned something from this lesson

*This is the end of this section. *

The Prophet and His Fruit: (Fruit of the Spirit)

"It is for freedom that Christ has set us free. Stand firm, then, and do not let yourselves be burdened again by a yoke of slavery." - Galatians 5:1 (NIV)

"Possess the fruit! Live unashamedly! Walk free!" - Ashley Reynolds

1. According to the Apostle Paul, we should: _____ in the _____, and we should not _____ the _____ of the _____. (Galatians 5:16).

2. Why does the flesh lust against the spirit and the spirit against the flesh? What is the purpose of this war?

_____

_____

_____. (Galatians 5:17)

3. According to Galatians 5:19-21, what are the works of the flesh? Using your bible dictionary, define these works:

1. Work: _____

Definition: _____

2. Work: _____

Definition: _____

3. Work: _____

Definition: _____

4. Work: _____

Definition: _____

5. Work: _____

Definition: _____

6. Work: _____

Definition: _____

7. Work: _____

Definition: _____

8. Work: _____

Definition: _____

9. Work: _____

Definition: _____

10. Work: _____

Definition: _____

11. Work: _____

Definition: _____

12. Work: _____

Definition: _____

13. Work: _____

Definition: _____

14. Work: _____

Definition: _____

15. Work: _____

Definition: _____

16. Work: _____

Definition: _____

17. Work: _____

Definition: _____

4. According to Galatians 5:21(b), will the people who choose to act out the works of the flesh inherit the kingdom of God? Explain your answer. _____ _____.

5. What is the kingdom of God according to the scriptures? "for the kingdom of God is not_____ and _____, but _____ and _____ and _____ in the Holy Ghost." (Romans 14:17) We can see that it's more to gain when operating in the kingdom than operating outside of it. When operating outside of this kingdom privilege you can only satisfy the flesh (eating and drinking), however, when you operate within this kingdom you access entrance into the spirit (peace, joy and righteousness). You satisfy your spirit man.

6. Where is this kingdom of God located? " nor will they say, "see here! or see there!" For indeed, the _____ is _____ you." (Luke 17:21)

7. What is the fruit of the spirit? Using your bible dictionary, define these fruits: (Galatians 5:22-23)

1. Fruit: _____

Definition: _____

2. Fruit: _____

Definition: _____

3. Fruit: _____

Definition: _____

4. Fruit: _____

Definition: _____

5. Fruit: _____

Definition: _____

6. Fruit: _____

Definition: _____

7. Fruit: _____

Definition: _____

8. Fruit: _____

Definition: _____

9. Fruit: _____

Definition: _____

7. Galatians 6:8 teaches us that: He who _____ to his _____ will of the _____ reap _____, but he who _____ to the spirit will of the _____ reap _____ _____.

Walking in the spirit is a choice just like living by the deeds of the flesh is a choice. As seen in this lesson, this is not easy and is a war. I want to encourage you that it is a battle that you can win with Christ on your side and the Holy Spirit within you.

8. And let us not grow _____ while doing good (walking in the fruit of the spirit), for in _____ _____ we shall _____ if we do not _____ _____. (Galatians 6:9)

9. I would beloved, that you choose the fruit of the spirit and not works of the flesh! Destroy the deeds of the flesh and live in the abundant life that God has prepared for you.

We hope that you have learned something from this lesson

*This is the end of this section. *

The Prophet and Rejection

"I tell you the truth, he continued, "no prophet is accepted in his hometown." - Luke 4:24 (NIV)

"Like the beetle unwelcomed in a fish tank and the pauper unwelcomed in a castle, so is the prophet the terrain of the heathen. However, just like there is a place for the beetle and the pauper, so is there a place for the prophet. It's in the presence of the Lord!" - Ashley Reynolds

1. Using your bible dictionary define rejection:

_____

_____.

2. According to the words of Jesus found in Luke 4:24, what did he say about prophets and rejection? "the He said, "Assuredly I say to you, no _____ is _____ in his own_____."

3. Luke 4:24 expresses that though the prophet is not accepted in his own country, it does not signify that he won't be accepted in order places.

4. With the spirit of rejection can come evil desire if the prophet does not stay in the presence of the Lord. Some of these evil desires can include:

1. Demonic isolation- a lure into secluded places that the devil has prepared

2. Sexual promiscuity

3. Idolatry- replacing God with other things

4. Overeating- your belly will become your god

5. Backslide- turn away from the Lord to satisfy your desire to feel accepted (drugs, alcohol, sex, etc.)

5. How will the prophet stay free from falling into such traps? Invite the spirit of God into your pain of rejection to help you cope: 2 Corinthians 3:17 "Where the _____of the _____ lord is there is _____."

6. Why does rejection visit the lives of the prophet? The spirit of rejection comes to attack the emotional well-being of the prophet. If he feels rejected of men, he will oftentimes wonder why he is alive. Afterall the prophetic ministry is for the people's sake. If people will not hear the prophet of reject his stance in the kingdom, the prophet will feel useless in the earth.

7. How can the prophet benefit form rejection?

      1. Spend more time with God

      2. Their ear gates can stay clearer   from negativity

3. Greater sensitivity of the movement of the spirit realm

4. More time spent knowing themselves

8. What can become some disadvantages of rejection?

1. Become spiritually blocked

2. Depression can settle in

3. Confused thoughts

4. Thoughts of taking your life

5. Disregarding your prophetic mantle

6. Abandoning your true self and taking on a false persona to be accepted

7. Turning to the things of this world to anthesize the pain associated with rejection

9. Do I have to fight these negative connotations alone? Absolutely not. However, prophets deal with a spirit of pride. When something is not well with them, they become too prideful to express what's going on with them for fear that it may damage their "prophetic" reputation. Know that you have help. Yes, you have God but know that he will also give you tangible help in the form of mentors, pastors. counselors, sisters, brothers, friends, etc. to help you through these seasons of your life.

10. I leave with you in this section some of the words that God gave me: "Behold I give unto you this day the power to doubt every doubt, curse every curse and to reject every rejection." Yes, you will be rejected, however what happens with this rejection totally depends on if you will accept it or reject it. Walk in your authority prophet. Choose to be free from the grips of rejection.

We hope that you have learned something from this lesson

*This is the end of this section. *

The Prophet and Suffering

"Jesus learned obedience through the things that he suffered." - Hebrews 5:8 : (NIV)

"Godly suffering has a reward. It is the gateway into power with God." - Ashley Reynolds

1. Young prophet please know that suffering at the will of God is not punishment for any wrongdoings on your behalf. This type of suffering is for the glory of God to be revealed in and through your life.

Let's examine what the scripture says about suffering

2. Romans 8:18, "for I consider that the _____ of this _____ _____ are not _____ to be compared with the _____ which shall be _____ in us."

This verse speaks of suffering with an "s"; this means that there are many sufferings that one will encounter. The good news is that this scripture also reveals that your suffering cannot be compared with what's next which is God's glory in your life.

3. Let's look at what some of these sufferings look like according to 2 Corinthians 12:10: " therefore I take pleasure in _____, in _____, in_____, in _____ and in _____ for _____ sake. For when I am _____, then I am _____."

It is my belief that this verse speaks of natural pains ushering one into supernatural sustainment. Though we are naturally suffering and feeling the effects of it' God will be strengthening us because we have a kingdom assignment to finish. These "things" cannot take us out or kill us because of the need that God will use us to fill.

4. Let's look at these sufferings or thorns significance: 2 Corinthians 12:7, " And lest I should be _____ above _____ by the abundance of the _____, a _____ in the _____ was given me, a message of _____ to _____ me, lest I be _____ above _____."

While Romans 8:18 reveals that suffering comes as a sign of "glory being revealed"; 2 Corinthians 12:7 shows us that our suffering or thorns are given because of the "revelations" shown us as well as to help keep us from "boasting".

5. This shows that while the sufferings do not feel good, it proves that it will work out for our good.

Romans 8:28 " And we _____ that _____ things work together for the _____ to those _____ love _____, to _____ who are the _____ according to his _____."

We have to trust that sometimes God's purpose for our lives is to suffer.

6. Isaiah 53:10 (NLT) : "But it was the _____ good plan to _____ him and cause him _____. Yet when his _____ is made an _____ for _____, he will have many _____. He will enjoy a _____ life, and the LORD's good plan will prosper in his hands. What this scripture shows us is that there is a benefit to suffering for God's sake.

7. Suffering is not designed to destroy you but it is to deliver you over into something greater. 2 Corinthians 4:8-9: We are hard _____, yet not _____; we are _____, but not in _____; persecuted, but not _____; struck _____, but not destroyed.

8. Suffering is to manifest Christ in us: 2 Corinthians 4:10-11

9. Know that you can make it through your suffering because God will prepare you: 2 Corinthians 5:5 "now He who has _____ for this very _____ is _____, who also has given us the _____ as a _____."

10. Read 2 Corinthians 4:17- you will find comfort to know that your suffering is light compared to the heaviness of the glory that shall rest on your life.

We hope that you have learned something from this lesson

*This is the end of this section. *

The Misunderstood Prophet

"Whoever gives heed to instruction prospers. And blessed is he who trusts in the Lord."
- Proverbs 16:20 (NIV)
"Prophets are normally questioned today, but figured out by tomorrow." - Ashley Reynolds

1. Prophets are not misunderstood because their words are inaccurate; they are misunderstood because most times the word does not sound logic to the human mind. Prophecy is not given for the human intellect. It can only be understood by the spirit of God.

2. When the prophet speaks, he is not aiming to appease to flesh or human intellect. He shows up to speak to the spirits of men.

3. The prophet is most times misunderstood and called crazy or a liar because most times what he speaks is delayed until a later time.

Let's examine some prophets who were misunderstood

4. 2 Kings 5:10, " and Elisha sent a _____ to him, saying "Go and _____ in the _____ _____ times, and your _____ shall be _____ to you, and you shall be _____.

Naaman was a man of valor and a leper. He wanted to be clean and so the prophet Elisha intervened after hearing about his plight. He gave him an uncommon instruction that he first rejected but after obeying, his prayers were answered.

5. The prophet Elisha gave an instruction to a widow whose back was against the wall with the debt that her husband left behind after his death. The creditors were scheduling to come and collect her 2 sons as collateral. She cried out to the prophet Elisha and he gave these instructions found in 2 Kings 4:3, "Then he said, "Go _____ vessels from _____, from all your _____, empty _____. Do not gather just a _____." This was a strange instruction only because the prophet wanted her to go borrow vessels when she was already in debt and trying to get out. It was also strange because he wanted her to go involve her neighbors (expose her trauma). Sometimes the very thing that we are trying to keep disclosed can be solved if we involve others. However, read 2 kings 4:4-7 and you will see that a misunderstood instruction led to her break-through.

6. Let's look at Jesus in Matthew 9:23-26 (NKJV) When Jesus came into the _____ _____ and saw the _____ _____ and then _____ _____ _____. (Vs 23) He said to them _____ _____, for them _____ is not _____, but _____. " And they _____ him. But when the _____ was put _____ He went in and _____ her by the hand and the _____ _____.

26

We can see that when prophets are misunderstood, they can be dismissed by people or like Jesus ridiculed. This only happens because the instructions that they speak sounds foolish. However, like the prophets of old we too must remain confident to know that no matter how foolish it may sound God will vindicate us by the manifestation of his word.

We hope that you have learned something from this lesson

*This is the end of this section. *

The Prophet and Paranoia

"Casting all thy care upon him for he cares for you." - 1 Peter 5:7 : (NIV)

"Like the levees hinder the flow of water; so, does paranoia blocks the prophetic flow." - Ashley Reynolds

1. Using your dictionary define the word: Paranoia

_____

_____.

2. It is to my understanding that the Spirit of paranoia comes to do 5 things:

1. To cause excessive worry

2. Disturb your inner peace

3. To hinder your destiny

4. To cause you to hide yourself away from society (not dealing with people)

5. To move you into desperation

3. 1 Kings 19:1 teaches us that the prophet Elijah had just finished doing a great work for the Lord and now he is overwhelmed by a spirit of paranoia due to Jezebel's threat. Let's look at 1 Kings 19:1, "And _____ told _____ all that _____ had done also how he had _____ all the _____ with the _____.

4. Young prophet I want you to know that it is typically after you do a major work for the Lord that you will be attacked by the forces of darkness. King Ahab and the false prophet Jezebel were dark hearted. 1 Kings 19:2, "Then _____ sent a messenger _____ to _____, saying, "So let the _____ do to me, and more also, if I do not make your _____ as the _____ of one of _____ by tomorrow about that time."

5. The intent of Jezebel's message to the prophet Elijah was to inflict fear and to cause him to be paralyzed in his faith. Let's look at how the prophet responded in 1 Kings 19:3-4 : " And when he saw that he arose and _____ for his _____, and went to Beersheba, which belongs to _____, and left his _____ there. (vs 3) But he himself went a day's journey into the _____, and came and sat down under a _____ tree. And he _____ that he might _____ and said, "It is enough! Now _____, take my _____, for I am _____ _____ than my father!"

6. It is a fact that God will give you a peace that will surpass all understanding. However, you must fulfill what 1 Peter 5:7 says: " _____ all of your _____ upon ____ for he _____ for you."

There comes a time in your life where you must learn to release all of your concerns and fears unto the Lord with an expectation that God has the power to relieve your soul and to bring you into freedom.

7. Proverbs 12:25: " _____ in the heart of _____ causes _____, But a _____ word makes it _____. "

We hope that you have learned something from this lesson

*This is the end of this section. *

The Logos and Rhema Word

" I have hidden your word in my heart that I might not sin against you." - Psalms 119:11 (NIV)

"The logos is the foundation from which the Rhema is derived." - Ashley Reynolds

1. Using you dictionary define these two words:

a. Logos:

_____.

b. Rhema:

_____.

2. According to the lesson on "the Logos and the Rhema word," which word can be changed and which word cannot be changed?

_____

_____.

3. In the lesson "The logos and the Rhema word, " we discussed how that a Rhema word is typically released in a spontaneous moment, which correlates with your present life situation. Let's examine in proverbs 15:23: "A man _____ has by the answer of his _____, and a _____ _____ in _____ _____, how good it is." When a Rhema word is spoken it is a on time word which brings clarity to a person's life in the moment.

4. In Matthew 4 :3-10, we see Jesus Christ standing on the logos word but not the Rhema word. Read Matthew 4:3-10, and express why you think that is.

_____

_____

_____

_____.

5. Matthew 4:4 says, "but he answered and said, "it is _____, "man shall not live by _____ alone but by every _____ that proceedeth from the _____ of _____.""

6. The purpose of this section was to express the difference between logos and rhema words. Though there is a difference, you need to know that they both hold significance and have a place in the lives of the believers.

We hope that you have learned something from this lesson

*This is the end of this section. *

The prophet and Word Practicality

"Be hearers and doers of the word of God." - James 1 :22 (NIV)

"The power is in the practice of the word." - Ashley Reynolds

1. Practicing the word of the Lord is what causes the prophet to access the power in Christ. There is nothing more that pleases God than to see a prophet of the Lord practicing his word.

2. The prophet David said, "I will _____ thy _____ Lord in _____ _____ that I might not _____ against _____ (psalms) This was right after David was restored from his sinful act of sexual sin with Bathsheba.

3. The Apostle James said in James 1:22, "But be _____ of the _____, and not _____ only, deceiving _____." Doing God's word helps you to store it in your memory lane so that you can remember to practice it. In doing so will you gain victory over your flesh and win over the devils' tactics in Jesus name.

4. While James 1:22 reveals to us a strategy on what we can do to gain victory over the devil, James 1:23-24 shows us what can happen to you when you don't keep the word constant before you. This will cause you to forget what manner of man God has created you to be. Read James 1:23-24.

5. The Apostle James shows us that our blessing is in "doing" the word: James 1:25, "But he who _____ into the _____ _____ of _____ and _____ in it, and is not a _____ _____ but a _____ of the work this one will be _____ in what he _____."

6. The Apostle Paul reminds us in Hebrews 4:2: "for indeed the _____ was _____ to us as well as to them; but the _____ which they heard did not _____ them not being _____ with _____ (action) in those who heard it." In order to see the word, move in our personal lives, we must mix it with action.

7. Hebrews 4:12, " for the _____ of _____ is _____ and _____, and _____ than any two-edged _____, piercing even to the _____ of _____ and _____, and of joints and marrow, and is a _____ of the _____ and _____ of the heart."

8.This lesson shows us that the word of God will work for us if we work it by "doing" it. It will cause us to live in constant victory through great discernment.

We hope that you have learned something from this lesson

*This is the end of this section. *

The Prophet and Offense

"And blessed is the one who is not offended by me."- Matthew 11:6 (ESV)

"Offense is only a thief of one's destiny. Choose today to be free and soar into your greatest prophetic height." - Ashley Reynolds

1. Using your bible dictionary define the word offense:

_____

_____.

2. According to the lesson "the prophet and offense," list 2 scriptures used to express what offense is and explain why you chose those two scriptures. How do you connect with these scriptures? What experiences do you have with them?

Scripture
1:_____

_____

Explanation:_____

_____

Scripture
2:_____

_____

Explanation:_____

_____

3. Name 2 of the signs that people display when they are offended according to the section on "The prophet and offense":

Offense sign # 1_____

Offense sign # 2_____

4. In 1Corinthians 8:9, the Apostle Paul talks about liberties. Why does he warn against us using our   liberty   amongst   those   who   are   weak?

_____

_____

_____.

5. In the lesson on "the prophet and offense" we talked about the different ways to handle offense with one of them being able to overlook it. Let's look at proverbs 19:11, " Good _____ makes one _____to _____, and it is his _____ to _____ an

_____." This simply means that for some offenses we don't need to address but we can simply overlook it while leaving it in the hands of the Lord.

6. In 2 Corinthians 6:3, the Apostle Paul teaches us why we should not cause offense. What is that
reason?_____

_____

_____.

7. It's good that we resolve offenses because it's hard to minister to and win one that is. Proverbs 18:19, " A _____ _____ is _____ to be won than a strong city, and _____ are like the bars of citadel."

8. read proverbs 10:12; and proverbs 17:9, and examine your heart. Take a moment and pray and ask God to show you if you love drama or like to walk in love.

9. Jesus said in " " that it is impossible to live without offense. However, I say it's your perspective and action towards it that counts the most. Selah! :)

We hope that you have learned something from this lesson

*This is the end of this section. *

The Prophet and the Scroll

"And he said to me, Son of man, eat what is before you, eat this scroll; then go and speak to the people of Israel. " - Ezekiel 3:1 (NIV)

"Before you can speak something you must first eat something." - Pastor V. Mainor

1. Using your bible dictionary, define the word scroll.

_____

_____.

Use the word scroll in a sentence.

_____

_____.

2. Moreover the Lord said to me, "_____ of _____, _____ what you find; _____ this _____, and _____, speak to the _____ of _____. (Ezekiel 3:1)

3. Note that the prophet was instructed to eat the scroll in order that he might do 2 things:

1. Go

2. Speak

4. Take note that in Ezekiel 3:1, the direction of Ezekiel's prophetic word was defined in that he was sent to the house of Israel. God will feed you (prophet) to the level that he intends to feed the people with whom you will be assigned to minister to.

5. It is not until you eat the scroll, that you will be empowered to prophetically do your assignment.

6. It will be the eating of the scroll to fill your belly that will give you sustaining power to stand strong against the great stubbornness of those you will be given a word for. Read Ezekiel 2:7-8)

7. 2 Timothy 2:15: "_____ to show yourself approved to _____, a _____ who does not need to be _____, _____ _____ the word of _____."

Notice that the whole point of you studying God's word is for God. You are aiming to prove to God that you are ready for him to use you. Studying God's word forms a greater level of confidence in you to bodily declare what thus says the Lord. The word of God has so many levels of understanding blessed is the one that draws it out through his pursuit of study.

8. Ezra gave himself _____ to the _____ of the law. Ezra was a priest called to teach Israel and he had to study. So, the prophet must dedicate himself over into the word so that he will be astute and qualified in his prophetic   ministry.

9. 1 Corinthians 14:29: "let two or three _____ speak, and let the _____ _____.

10. I laugh because I am at my desk @ work and I went into a vision. I saw the prophet working for the word and when he stood up to preach the scroll spoke out and began to work for him. Young prophet if you decide to sit down in this word privately you will never be put to shame publicly. Selah! :)

We hope that you have learned something from this lesson

*This is the end of this section. *

The prophet and his Faith

"And the just shall live by his faith." - Habakkuk 2:4 (b) (NIV)

"If you can get faith; you can get anything." - Ashley Reynolds

1. Take the next 30 seconds and declare out of your mouth these words: "my faith is taking me somewhere."

2. "Now _____ is the _____ of things _____ for; the _____ of things not _____." (Hebrews 11:1)

3. "But the _____ shall_____by _____ _____." (Habakkuk 2:4 (b)

4. Think back in your mind of something that you had to believe God to do by faith
_____
_____.

5. What was the faith process like for you?
_____
_____
_____.

6. How did receiving what you had faith for God to do increase your faith level?
_____
_____
_____.

7. "And seeing their faith, Jesus said to the man on the mat, your sins are forgiven, rise pick up your mat and walk." () According to this scripture do you feel that someone can be healed or made whole off of the faith level of someone else?
_____
_____
_____
_____.

8. Read Hebrews 11. List 8 people who had faith and how having faith benefitted them/others:

　　1.　Person: _____
　　　　Benefit:_____

　　2.　Person: _____
　　　　Benefit:_____

3. Person: _____
   Benefit:_____

4. Person: _____
   Benefit:_____

5. Person: _____
   Benefit:_____

6. Person: _____
   Benefit:_____

7. Person: _____
   Benefit:_____

8. Person: _____
   Benefit:_____

We hope that you have learned something from this lesson

*This is the end of this section. *

The Prophet and Rest

"He makes me to lie down in green pastures; he leads me besides the still waters."
-Psalms 23 :2 (NIV)

"It is in the restful meadows that we can hear Gods still small voice clearer." - Ashley Reynolds

1. Rest in Christ is your pathway into a more meaningful and effective prophetic ministry.

2. Philippians 4:7 (NKJV) :" And the _____ of _____, which surpasses all _____, will guard your _____ and _____ through Christ Jesus."

3. Proverbs 1:33 (NKJV), "But whoever _____ to me will _____ safely and will be _____, without _____ of _____." When you listen to the instructions of God to rest, he will keep you secure and you will have no fear of evil. God will keep you from the demonic grips of paranoia.

4. Psalms 107:29, (NKJV): "He calms the _____ so that its _____ are _____." When we rest in God, he will cause whatever was turbulent in our lives to be still. He will cause there to be an inner rest/peace.

5. The prophet David expresses how the Lord led him into rest in psalms 23:2, "He _____ me to _____ down in _____ _____. He _____ me beside the _____ waters."

6. The prophet Isaiah consoles " " in that it is the will of God that he grants them rest from their hard labor. Let's examine Isaiah 14:3, "it shall come to pass in the _____ the _____ gives you _____ from your _____ and from your _____ and the _____ _____ in which you were made to _____."

7. Isaiah 26:4, " _____ (rest) in the _____ forever, for in _____ the Lord, is _____ _____." This rest in God is sure to strengthen you for the journey ahead.

8. When God is with you, he will do 2 things for you according to Exodus 33:14

1. give you his presence

2. give you his rest

9. Resting in God will give you a reprieve from the constant prophetic demands and battles that you will encounter during your prophetic reign. Let's look at Exodus 14:14, " The _____ will _____ for you, and _____ shall _____ for your _____."

We hope that you have learned something from this lesson

*This is the end of this section. *

The Prophets Rank

Where does it come from?

"Before I formed you in the womb I knew you, before you were born I set you apart I appointed you as a prophet to the nations." - Jeremiah 1:5 (NIV)

"Let Gods hand establish you prophetically. In this will you be given your true prophetic authority." - Ashley Reynolds

1. According to the Lesson "The prophets Rank; Where does it come from?", who gives the prophet his rank in the kingdom?

_____

_____.

2. In Jeremiah 1:5, who had ordained Jeremiah to be a prophet?

_____

_____.

3. Jeremiah 1:5, discloses the expansion of Jeremiah's prophetic reach. To whom was Jeremiah called to be a prophetic voice?

_____

_____.

4. According to the Lesson "The prophets Rank; Where does it come from?", what will God do in order to help the prophet not run before his time?

_____

_____.

5. In your bible dictionary, look up the word zealous. What does it mean?

_____

_____.

6. How does this word, zealous, relate to budding prophets?

_____

_____

_____.

7. According to the Lesson "The prophets Rank; Where does it come from?", why shouldn't we allow for people to give us rank but should wait on the Lord for our prophetic establishment?_____

_____

_____

_____.

We hope that you have learned something from this lesson

*This is the end of this section. *

The Prophet and his Flaws

"9 Do you not know that the unrighteous will not inherit the kingdom of God? Do not be deceived. Neither fornicators, nor idolaters, nor adulterers, nor [a]homosexuals, nor [b]sodomites, 10 nor thieves, nor covetous, nor drunkards, nor revilers, nor extortioners will inherit the kingdom of God..."- 1 Corinthians 6:9-10, (NKJV)

"Having flaws can at times become the gravity that connects you with God."- Ashley Reynolds

1. According to the lesson: "The prophet and his Flaws," what are flaws?_____

_____.

2. Are prophets the only people that have flaws or does every human have them?_____

_____.

3. According to the lesson: "The prophet and his Flaws," Where do flaws arise from?

_____

_____

_____.

4. Are flaws a sign that you are in the wrong standing with God or is it a part of your human experience?

5. 1 Corinthians 6:9-11: "or do you not know that the unrighteous will not inherit the _____ of _____? Do not be deceived: neither the _____ immoral, nor _____, nor _____, nor men who practice_____. nor _____, nor the_____, nor _____, nor _____, nor _____ will inherit the kingdom of God. And such were some of _____. But you were _____, you were ____, you were _____ in the name of the Lord _____ _____ and by the _____ of our God."

6. Exodus 4:10, " Moses said to the Lord, _____ your servant, Lord. I have never been _____, neither in the past nor since you have _____ to your servant. I am _____ of _____ and _____."

7. Let's look at the flaws of some other prophets and leaders chosen by the Lord:

   a. **Person:** Apostle Paul

   b. **Flaw:** Murderer- Paul persecuted the Jews

   c. **Scripture reference:** Acts 8:1-3; Acts 26: 9-11 (NKJV)

d. **Delivered:** Yes

a. **Person:** Jonah

b. **Flaw:** Disobedient and unmerciful- Jonah rebelled against preaching to God's people because he felt as if they did not deserve another chance

c. **Scripture reference:** Jonah 1 :1-3

d. **Delivered:** Yes

a. **Person:** Miriam

b. **Flaw:** Arrogant- Prophetess Miriam was arrogant in her approach towards her leader (Moses)

c. **Scripture reference:** Numbers 12:1 (NKJV)

d. **Delivered:** Yes

a. **Person:** David

b. **Flaw:** Adulterer- King/Prophet David had sex with Bathsheba. She was not his wife

c. **Scripture reference:** 2 Samuel 11 :1-4 (NKJV)

d. **Delivered:** Yes

8. There is a flaw that you will never find deliverance from. This is found in the life of Esau:

b. **Flaw:** Blasphemy against the Holy Ghost- This is arrogance towards God or sacred things; it is a lack of reverence

c. **Scripture reference:** Genesis 27:34-40; Hebrews 12:17

d. **Delivered:** No

9. It matters not what your flaws are. You can be set free. God has chosen you for a time such as this. Ask God to help you with your flaws and decide today to walk in your prophetic calling.

We hope that you have learned something from this lesson

*This is the end of this section. *

The Prophet and the Spirit of Greed

" For the love of money is a root of all kinds of evil, for which some have strayed from the faith in their greediness, and pierced themselves through with many sorrows."
- 1 Timothy 6:10, (NKJV)

"The truth behind this spirit of Greed is that it preys upon the lack and dissatisfaction of one. It's not that they do not have. It's just that they are discontent. I challenge you to find contentment in your inner man and be free from greed."- Ashley Reynolds

1. According to the Lesson, "the prophet and the spirit of greed," what is the spirit of greed?

_____

_____

_____.

2. In the Lesson "the prophet and the spirit of greed," what are some examples that the spirit of greed will have you overly desirous for?

_____

_____

_____.

3. According to the Lesson, "the prophet and the spirit of greed," what is "ungodly" greed?

_____

_____.

What is "godly"
greed?_____

_____.

4. 1 Timothy 6:10, "The _____ of _____ is the _____ of _____kinds of _____." This scripture proves that it is because of the love for money (greed) that people will entertain other spiritual wickedness for the purpose of having what they desire.

5. According to the Lesson, "the prophet and the spirit of greed," what are 2 of the spirits that usually accompany the spirit of greed?

1. _____

2. _____

6. According to the Lesson, "the prophet and the spirit of greed," how does these 2 spirits operate in a person? (Ezekiel 22:12-read)

1.

_____

_____

2.

_____

_____

7. Read proverbs 1:19: "What can the greedy spirit lead a person to do?

_____

_____

_____.

8. "The _____ of the _____ killeth him; for his hands refuse to _____. He coveth_____ all the day long; but the _____ giveth and spareth not. " (Read proverbs 21:25-26 NKJV)

9. As a prophet of God you need to know that God has already given you everything you need to be sufficient (1 Cor 9:) you have no need to be greedy. It will only lead to destruction.

We hope that you have learned something from this lesson

*This is the end of this section. *

The Voice of the Prophet

"The voice of one crying in the wilderness: "Make straight the way of the Lord."- John 1:23, (NKJV)

"The amplitude of your prophetic voice is not in words only but also in deeds. Cry loud and spare not."- Ashley Reynolds

1. As a prophet, you must realize that you are a voice that has been given a sphere by God to prophetically shape, mold and prepare his people to engage Christ.

2. In the lesson, "The Prophet and his Voice," we learned that when Jesus spoke the words he had spoken were spirit and life, what was he really saying?

    1. My words are spirit:

    _____
    _____
    _____

    2. And life:

    _____
    _____
    _____

3. What did the prophet John the Baptist answer with when asked by the Jews, priest and Levites, "what do you say about yourself? (Read John 1:23 NKJV)

_____
_____
_____.

4. According to the lesson, "The Prophet and his Voice," why are prophetic voices given?

_____
_____
_____

5. According to the lesson, "The Prophet and his Voice," what 6 prophetic authorities can a true prophetic voice perform as found in Jeremiah 1:10?

1.

2.

3.

4.

5.

6.

How many of these prophetic authorities are destructive? _____

How many of these prophetic authorities are constructive? _____

This shows us that prophets should be careful of what they release out of their mouths as concerns themselves and others. In your mouth lies the ability to destroy or to build.

6. If your prophetic voice has both destructive and constructive ability, why should the prophet be   cautious   of   the   words   that   come   out   of   his/her   mouth?
_____
_____
_____
_____.

7. According to the lesson, "The Prophet and his Voice," we learned in the story of Balaam and Balak that we as prophets do not use our prophetic voice abilities to abuse people or to speak word curses. This is why the prophet should discern the spirit in which they are about to speak to see if it be of God or of their own divisive agenda. Selah.

We hope that you have learned something from this lesson

*This is the end of this section. *

Displaced Prophets

"but you came back, ate bread, and drank water in the place of which the Lord said to you, "Eat no bread and drink no water," your corpse shall not come to the tomb of your fathers." -1 King 13:22 (NKJV)

"Like a clam which houses pearls is of no value outside its element of water, so is the prophet outside of his prophetic element."- Ashley Reynolds

1. According to the lesson "Displaced Prophets," what does being displaced mean?

_____

_____

_____.

2. In the Lesson "Displaced Prophets," we learned how that for the prophet being displaced meant being out of range in 3 areas:

1.

2.

3.

3. In the Lesson "Displaced Prophets," we learned how that for the displaced prophet, he or she could start trying to do lots of "works" in order to feel

_____

_____.

4. According to the lesson, "Displaced Prophets," name 2 of the 4 ways that being in your prophetic place can help you and your ministry:

1.

2.

Why did you choose these 2? In what way/s do you relate with these?

_____

_____

_____

_____

_____

_____

_____.

5. According to the Lesson "Displaced Prophets," name (2) of the (4) ways that being displaced can hinder your prophetic ministry.

1.

2.

Why did you choose these 2
hinderances?_____

_____

_____

_____

_____.

6. Sense knowing that you were a prophet, have you ever felt displaced? Explain yourself.

_____

_____

_____

_____

_____.

We hope that you have learned something from this lesson

*This is the end of this section. *

The Focused Prophet

" Now it came to pass, when the time had come for Him to be received up, that He steadfastly set His face to go to Jerusalem." - Luke 9:51 (NKJV)

"The prophet's ability to focus throughout his prophetic journey will ensure the success he or she desires."- Ashley Reynolds

1. According to the lesson, "The Focused Prophet," how can focus be defined?_____

_____

_____.

2. According to the lesson, "The Focused Prophet," The _____ must become _____ of the _____ that he feels _____ is _____ him.

3. Luke 9:51 (NKJV), "Now it came to pass when the _____ had come for him to be _____ up, that he _____ set his face to _____ to _____."

4. According to the lesson, "The Focused Prophet," we discussed focus as it relates to Habakkuk 2:2. Do you agree with what was said about focus as it relates to Habakkuk 2:2? Or do you have another opinion? Express yourself.

_____

_____

_____

_____

_____

_____

_____

5. Habakkuk 2:2, "Then the Lord answered me and said: "_____ the _____ and make it _____ on _____; that he may run who _____ it." What this scripture does is that it helps us to know that in order to be focused enough to write anything as prophetic scribes we must first become focused enough to hear God on what to write.

6. Proverbs 4:1, "_____, my children, the _____ of a _____ and give _____ to know _____."

7. Solomon, the teacher of wisdom declares, "my _____, keep my _____, and _____ my _____ within _____. Keep my _____ and live, and my _____ as the _____ of your _____." (Proverbs 7:1-2) This shows us that focus on the words of God bring life.

8. According to the lesson, "The Focused Prophet," name the (4) disruptions of prophetic focus:

1.

2.

3.

4.

9. Which one/s of these do you find yourself wrestling with the most at times?

_____ _____

_____

_____

_____

_____.

10. I challenge you to pray this prayer and then ask God to help you develop a personal plan to combat lack of focus.

We hope that you have learned something from this lesson

*This is the end of this section. *

The Secluded Prophet

"Before I formed you in the womb, I knew[a] you, and before you were born, I set you apart. I appointed you to be a prophet to the nations.."- Jeremiah 1:5 (EHV)- *Divine Seclusion*

"There Elijah went into a cave and stayed all night. Then the Lord spoke his word to him: "Elijah! Why are you here?"- 1 Kings 19:9 (NCV) - *Demonic Seclusion*

"Seclusion can be to the prophets benefit or to his detriment."- Ashley Reynolds

1. Using your bible dictionary what does the word seclusion mean?

_____

_____

_____.

Use the word seclusion in a sentence

_____

_____

2. According to the lesson "The secluded prophet," we learned that: some _____ were _____ ordained and used as a means of _____ and _____. However, other reasons or seclusion were demonic.

3. According to the lesson "The secluded prophet," what were the other reasons that the prophet was drawn to seclusion?

    1.

    2.

    3.

4. According to the lesson "The secluded prophet," what will the devil speak to the mind of the prophet if they seclude themselves while battling against hurt, pain, offense, etc.:

_____

_____

_____.

5. Take 15 minutes to read 1 Kings 18 and 1 Kings 19. You will see how the prophet Elijah is used by the Lord to bring death and destruction to the false house of Ahab and Jezebel. However,

read 1 Kings 19:1-4 carefully to see how the Lords prophet chooses to seclude himself away from society in order to abandon his fear of having to face Jezebel.

6. 1 Kings 19:2 :then _____ (Elijah's enemy that inflicted intimidation upon him) sent a _____to _____, saying, "so let the _____ do to me and more also, if I do not make your _____ as the _____ of one of them by _____ about this time. "

Let's look at how the prophet of God secludes himself in 1 Kings 19:3:

7. " And when he saw that, he _____ and _____for his _____, and went to _____ (means) which belongs to Judah, and _____ his _____ there." We can see that the prophet starts to do 2 things:

   1. pray out of alignment of what God's will was for his life. God was not ready for him to join his fathers who were dead and buried

   2. This fear of Jezebel caused the prophet to ask for an untimely death. This is what happens to those of us who are secluded away from people who can give us strength on account of our own fears, pain, hurts, etc. We will start to desire that God grants us our own selfish wish by taking away our natural life or our spiritual prophetic abilities.

8. Some God ordained seclusions can be found in the lives of:

   1. Jeremiah- Was called by God to live a consecrated life unto him having not married or having children

   2. John the Baptist- lived in the wilderness where he was trained by the Holy Spirit on how to love God, hear his voice and to spend time with the Holy spirit to become more prophetically keen in the spirit.

   3. David- A shepherd's boy whom the Lord hid in the desert until an appointed time

We hope that you have learned something from this lesson

*This is the end of this section. *

The Persecuted Prophet

"Jerusalem, Jerusalem, who kills the prophets and stones those who are sent to her."
-Matthew 23: 37, (CSB)
"Persecution for the prophet is more so a sign from God that they are on the right track."- Ashley Reynolds

1. O Jerusalem, Jerusalem, who _____ the _____ and _____ those sent to her, how often I have longed to gather your children together, as a hen gathers her chicks under her wings, but you were unwilling! (Matthew 23:37-BSB)

2. According to the lesson, "The Persecuted Prophet," which ministry gift is persecuted the most?

_____

_____

Why do you think this ministry gift is mostly persecuted?

_____

_____

_____

3. According to the lesson, "The Persecuted Prophet," what does it mean to be persecuted?

_____

_____

_____

4. Have you ever been persecuted? If so, explain why you think this happened to you and how it made you feel. If you have not experienced persecution, just wait because you will be. It's a part of the prophetic call.

_____

_____

_____

_____

_____

5. In the lesson, "The Persecuted Prophet," who are they that are more likely to persecute the prophet? (Read Jeremiah 1:18)

      1.

      2.

      3.

4.

6. According to the lesson, "The Persecuted Prophet," we learned through Ezekiel 3:7 that the persecution is really against who?

_____

_____.

- According to the lesson, "The Persecuted Prophet," we learned through the life of Daniel how sometimes you will be persecuted as a prophet on account of your choice to serve God while others are not. (Read Daniel 6- CEV)

We hope that you have learned something from this lesson

*This is the end of this section. *

The Prophet and People

"One who has unreliable friends soon comes to ruin, but there is a friend who sticks closer than a brother." Proverbs 18:24, (NIV)

"Life is good when you let people in. Selah"- Ashley Reynolds

1. Let's look at David and Jonathans relationship in 1 Samuel 18:1-4 (ESV): "As soon as he had finished speaking to Saul, the soul of Jonathan was knit to the soul of David, and Jonathan loved him as his own soul. 2 And Saul took him that day and would not let him return to his father's house. 3 Then Jonathan made a covenant with David, because he loved him as his own soul. 4 And Jonathan stripped himself of the robe that was on him and gave it to David, and his armor, and even his sword and his bow and his belt. 5 And David went out and was successful wherever Saul sent him, so that Saul set him over the men of war. And this was good in the sight of all the people and also in the sight of Saul's servants."

In these verses we can see how David's life goes to another level as rising king due to having Jonathan as a part of his life.

2. According to the lesson "The Prophet and People," prophets can walk _____ but not be _____.

3. According to the lesson "The Prophet and People," God has made us _____ and _____ beings.

4. According to the lesson "The Prophet and People," A part of our holistic health involves what?

_____
_____
_____

5. What is considered unhealthy thinking according to the lesson, "The Prophet and People,"?

_____

_____

6. Luke 2 :44, (ESV) "44 but supposing Him to have been in the company, they went a day's journey, and sought Him among their _____ and _____ .

This verse reveals that even Jesus had friends. In my opinion this shows how that Jesus did not embrace the lie that he was "too good or too high" to have friends. No! Jesus had friends. Ask God for true friend's young prophet. When you get them do not only expect them to build you but you find ways to build them. This can be done through words of encouragement, acknowledgement, money gifts, support, etc. True friends enter one another's life to discern what is needed and then they seek God as to what they can do to fill it. Do not allow the enemy to make you think that your only true friend is in God. God has a person/s in the flesh that will be God ordained to do life with you. Selah! :)

7. According to the lesson "The Prophet and People," why should the prophet allow God to choose   his   or   her   "people"   connections?

_____

_____

_____

_____

8. Relationships are two dimensional. Why is it important for both the prophet and his/her friends   to   add   positively   to   one   another   while   in   relationship?

_____

_____

_____?

9. Young prophet be content with knowing that you are not made to walk this earth alone. You will find yourself flourishing when you are healthy and when you allow other healthy people into your space. Selah. :)

10. Proverbs 18:24 (NIV) says, "One who has _____ friends soon come to _____, but there is a _____ who sticks closer than a brother. This scripture shows us that in this life there are some relationships that you will have that will not only come from your blood line, but they will develop from people who are not in your bloodline.

11. Young prophet, you need a friend. Let people in! Selah.

We hope that you have learned something from this lesson

*This is the end of this section. *

The Warfare of the Prophet

"You have seen the depth of their vengeance all their plots against me. Lord, you have heard their insults, all their plots against me what my enemies whisper and mutter against me all day long." -Lamentations 3:60-62 (NIV)

"The warfare of the prophet happens during the beginning, middle and just before the brink of word fulfillment."- Ashley Reynolds

1. In the lesson "The warfare of the prophet," who was it that established the ministry of the prophet to be a part of the body of Christ because it is necessary?

_____

_____

_____

2. According to the Lesson, "The warfare of the prophet," what was the one major advantage that prophets bring to the body of Christ?

_____

_____

_____

3. According to the Lesson, "The warfare of the prophet," prophets must _____ with what _____ reveals to them as relates to _____ . (3:3)

4. According to the Lesson, "The warfare of the prophet," what is Ashley Reynolds saying about prophets?

_____

_____ :)

5. In the lesson "The Warfare of the Prophet," we learned that in the prophets lies _____ _____ of _____ heart. You are special young prophet because you have God's heart.

6. According to the Lesson, "The warfare of the prophet," who is Lucifer and what happened to him?

_____

_____

_____

7. According to the Lesson, "The warfare of the prophet," what was the most taunting reality of Lucifer's dethroning?

_____

_____

_____

8. Satan can _____ be _____ from the sure _____ of the lake of fire nor the _____ of hell.

9. At the end of prophetic warfare, we found out that it truly is an attack on who? God or the prophet? Explain:

_____

_____

_____

_____

_____

10. According to the Lesson, "The warfare of the prophet," what are the 3 dimensions of prophetic warfare? Explain your answers:

1.

2.

3.

We hope that you have learned something from this lesson

*This is the end of this section. *

Major Spirits that Attack the Prophets

" Remember my affliction and roaming, The wormwood and the gall. My soul still remembers And sinks within me. This I recall to my mind, Therefore I have hope. Through the Lord's mercies we are not consumed, Because His compassions fail not. They are new every morning; Great is Your faithfulness. "The Lord is my portion," says my soul, Therefore I hope in Him!" - Lamentations 3:19-24 (NKJV)

"There is not an attack from the devil that God does not have the power to deliver you from."- Ashley Reynolds

1. According to the lesson " Major Spirits that Attack the Prophets," is the prophet without hope when dealing with any attack from the devil? Explain:

_____

_____

_____

2. List the (6) spirits listed in the lesson, "Major Spirits that Attack the Prophets," that attack prophets the most:

1.

2.

3.

4.

5.

6.

3. Of these 6 spirits, which one/s have you found yourself wrestling with the most?

_____

_____

Why do you think this is? (be honest)

_____

_____

_____

4. Take a moment to repeat this prayer: "Lord I realize that I am under attack by the spirit/s of _____ (you fill in the blank)." "Father, I come to you because I am in need of breakthrough. I no longer want this spirit/s to antagonize my very soul. Deliver me Lord. I believe that you have the power to set me

free. I give you permission to enter into my soul and to cut away every seed that this spirit/s have sown. I receive from you oh Lord and I chose to walk in my freedom. In Jesus' mighty name I pray. Amen."

5. Why do you think the devil attacks God's prophets with the spirits listed in the lesson, "Major Spirits   that   Attack   the   Prophets?"

_____

_____

_____

_____

_____

_____

6. I encourage you to download music from Psalmist Raine onto your mp3 player. Every time you sense a demonic force rising to antagonize your soul, play this music and begin praying and you will see how that the glory of the Lord will descend into your soul and bring the freedom sought after.

We hope that you have learned something from this lesson

*This is the end of this section. *

The Person Outside of the Prophetic

"Before I formed you in the womb I knew you; Before you were born I sanctified[a] you; I [b]ordained you a prophet to the nations."- Jeremiah 1:5 (NKJV)

"Aside from your prophetic abilities, there is you."- Ashley Reynolds

1. "Then _____ said, "Let Us make _____ in Our _____, according to Our _____; let them have _____ over the fish of the sea, over the birds of the air, and over the cattle, over [a]all the earth and over every creeping thing that creeps on the earth."- Genesis 1:26 (NKJV)

2. "Before _____ formed _____ in the womb _____ knew _____; Before _____ were born _____ sanctified _____ ; _____ ordained you a _____ to the _____ (Jeremiah 1:5-NKJV)

3. Read Jeremiah 1:5. We can see the order in which God deals with Jeremiah:

    1. He spent time knowing him (as a person)

    2. He separated him (for service)

    3. God finally decided to ordain Jeremiah as (prophet)

4. According to the lesson, "The Person outside of the Prophetic," we learned that most people introduce the _____ of who they are instead of the _____.

5. One reason that people shine what they do before who they are is because they want to be _____ by men.

6. Do you feel as though what you **DO** is more important than who you **ARE**? Explain your answer:

_____

_____

_____

_____

_____

_____

_____

7. How does knowing who you are as a person help with your prophetic calling?

_____

_____

_____

_____

_____

_____

_____

8. Beside each word listed, identify if it is a _verb_ or an _adjective_. (Reminder: verb = "what you **DO'**); (adjectives = "who you **ARE"**)

1. Preacher_____

2. Teacher_____

3. Loving_____

4. Authoritative_____

5. Kind_____

6. Prophet_____

7. Prophesy_____

8. Tall_____

9. Father_____

10. Teach_____

11. Short_____

12. Dark_____

13. Light_____

14. Preach_____

How did you do?

_____

Now that you are able to correctly separate who you are from what you do; describe who you are:_____

_____

_____

_____

_____

9. Young prophet, always know that you are valuable as a person.

We hope that you have learned something from this lesson

*This is the end of this section. *

Different Forms of Prophecy

"Long ago, at many times and in many ways, God spoke to our fathers by the prophets,"
Hebrews 1:1 (ESV)

"Prophecy is unique in that it is multi-dimensional"- Ashley Reynolds

1. According to the Lesson, "Different Forms of Prophecy," we learned that there are 3 different forms of prophetic utterances; What are they:

     1. _____

     2. _____

     3. _____

2. According to the Lesson, "Different Forms of Prophecy," how can Word of knowledge be defined? Word of knowledge is when someone _____ _____ about someone by way of the _____ of the _____ _____.

3. According to the Lesson, "Different Forms of Prophecy," word of knowledge is something that you could _____ have known unless it was shared with you by the _____ of _____.

4. In the Lesson, "Different Forms of Prophecy," wisdom can be linked to what?
_____

5. In wisdom can be found the _____ of what we should do after recieving a word of knowledge.

6. In the Lesson, "Different Forms of Prophecy," What is a word of prophecy?
_____
_____

7. According to the Lesson, "Different Forms of Prophecy," Identify which form of prophetic utterance deal with: Past, present or future:

1. Word of Knowledge-

2. Word of Wisdom-

3. Word of Prophecy-

8. After reading the section on, "Different Forms of Prophecy," Which form of prophecy do you feel God uses you the most?

_____

_____

_____

_____

_____

_____

We hope that you have learned something from this lesson

*This is the end of this section. *

Different Types of Prophets

"But by the grace of God I am what I am, and his grace toward me was not in vain. On the contrary, I worked harder than any of them, though it was not I, but the grace of God that is with me"- 1 Corinthians 15:10 (ESV)

"While all prophets have the same gift: their approaches to the gift will be different. "- Ashley Reynolds

1. According to the lesson on the different types of prophets, we learned that all prophets are

_____

2. According to the lesson, "Different Types of Prophets," list and explain 6 of the different types discussed:

1. Prophetic type: _____
   Explanation:_____

   _____
   _____
   _____

2. Prophetic type: _____
   Explanation:_____

   _____
   _____
   _____

3. Prophetic type: _____
   Explanation:_____

   _____
   _____
   _____

4. Prophetic type: _____
   Explanation:_____

   _____
   _____
   _____

5. Prophetic type: _____
   Explanation:_____

   _____
   _____
   _____

6. Prophetic type: _____

   Explanation:_____
   _____
   _____
   _____

3. In the lesson, "Different Types of Prophets," We learned that it is because prophets are unique that they cannot be _____.

4. According to the lesson, "Different Types of Prophets," Answer the following questions:

   a. Priestly Prophet:

       How do they function:
       _____
       _____
       _____
       _____

       Example:
       _____
       _____
       _____
       _____

       Can you Identify?:
       _____
       _____
       _____
       _____

   b. Kingly Prophet:

       How do they function:
       _____
       _____
       _____

       Example:
       _____
       _____

_____

_____

Can you Identify?:

_____

_____

_____

_____

c. Shepherdly Prophet:

How do they function:

_____

_____

_____

_____

Example:

_____

_____

_____

_____

Can you Identify?:

_____

_____

_____

_____

d. Governmental Prophet:

How do they function:

_____

_____

_____

_____

Example:

_____

_____

_____

_____

Can you Identify?:

_____

_____
_____
_____

e. Intercessory Prophet:

How do they function:

_____
_____
_____
_____

Example:

_____
_____
_____
_____

Can you Identify?:

_____
_____
_____
_____

f. Military Prophet:

How do they function:

_____
_____
_____
_____

Example:

_____
_____
_____
_____

Can you Identify?:

_____
_____
_____
_____

g. Deliverance Prophet:

How do they function:

_____
_____
_____
_____

Example:

_____
_____
_____
_____

Can you Identify?:

_____
_____
_____
_____

h. Birthing Prophet:

How do they function:

_____
_____
_____
_____

Example:

_____
_____
_____
_____

Can you Identify?:

_____
_____
_____
_____

i. Evangelical Prophet:

How do they function:

_____
_____

_____

Example:

_____

_____

_____

Can you Identify?:

_____

_____

_____

_____

5. After reading and studying about the different types of prophets have you been able to identify with what type of prophet you are?

Yes _____   or   No _____

6. Which type of prophet do you identify the most with from the bible?

_____

_____

_____

_____

7. If neither of the types of prophets discussed in this lesson have identified with how you feel you are as a prophet, express what type of prophet you feel that you are with a scriptural reference:

Type of prophet: _____

Scriptural reference:

_____

_____

_____

_____

_____

8. According to 1 Corinthians 15:10 (ESV), the prophet should never box themselves into one facet of the prophetic ministry. This is because God can choose to change how he uses you as a prophet at any time. It's whatever the grace that he extends upon your life.

"But by the _____ of _____ I am what I am, and his _____ toward me was not in _____. On the contrary, I worked harder than any of them, though it was not I, but the _____ of _____ that is with me."

9. Whatever type of prophet you are, it is my sincere prayer that you grow healthily in it and that God will take you places that you could only imagine. Stay close to God and under your leader/ mentor. I love you.

We hope that you have learned something from this lesson

*This is the end of this section. *

Signs of a Chosen Prophet

"For the Lord God does nothing without revealing his secret to his servants the prophets."- Amos 3:7 (ESV)

"True prophets are not as interested in being served as much as they live to serve both God and his people."- Ashley Reynolds

1. In the lesson, "Signs of a Chosen Prophet," what did you learn about what it means to be chosen by the Lord?

_____
_____
_____
_____

2. Can you remember the time when you were brought into the enlightenment of knowing that you were a prophet? Yes _____   or   No _____

3. If you chose "No," I encourage you to keep seeking the Lord. If you chose "Yes," share your experience?

_____
_____
_____
_____
_____
_____
_____

4. Now that you know that you are a prophet of God, do you surround yourself with other prophetic company? You must know that as a prophet of God, your company must match who you are and where you are going._____
_____
_____
_____
_____

5. In the lesson, "Signs of a Chosen Prophet," we defined 11 signs of being a Prophet of God. List the 6 top signs that you have experienced and why you chose these?

    a. Sign _____

       Why you chose this:

       _____

       _____

       _____

    b. Sign _____

       Why you chose this:

       _____

       _____

       _____

    c. Sign _____

       Why you chose this:

       _____

       _____

       _____

    d. Sign _____

       Why you chose this:

       _____

       _____

       _____

    e. Sign _____

       Why you chose this:

       _____

       _____

       _____

    f. Sign _____

       Why you chose this:

       _____

       _____

       _____

6. "For the Lord God does _____ without revealing his secret to his _____ the prophets."- Amos 3:7 (ESV) This verse reveals that God will gladly open his secrets to those

prophets who are humble. When God sees your servitude spirit, he will draw nearer to you and allow for you to have access to his hearts

7. This brings me to my next point in that another sign that is associated with true prophets of the Lord is that they have the heart of God. Yes, the heart of God is open to these.

8. I encourage each of you to not depend on having a sign more so than hearing the voice of God to tell you that you are his prophet or prophesier. When you get this confirmation, allow the Holy Spirit to guide you on how you should be used in this prophetic calling. I love you all.

We hope that you have learned something from this lesson

*This is the end of this section. *

The Prophet and Emotionalism

"Jesus Wept!"- John 11:35 (NIV)

"Weeping truly endures but for a night, but joy is sure to spring forth at the rising of the sun! "- Ashley Reynolds

1. Emotions can be defined as a _____ instinctive state of _____ deriving from one's _____, _____, or _____ with others.

2. In the lesson, "The Prophet and Emotionalism," we learned that emotions can deceive you if you are not careful. What do you think this really means?_____

_____

_____

_____

3. In the lesson, "The Prophet and Emotionalism," we learned that there are 3 things that emotions can do for us:

    1. _____

    2. _____

    3. _____

4. Why does the bible tell us to cast all of our cares upon him?

_____

_____

_____

_____

_____

5. In the lesson, "The Prophet and Emotionalism," there is a list of things that can happen as a sign that you are under emotional attack. What are they?:

    1. _____

2. _____

3. _____

4. _____

5. _____

6. _____

7. _____

6. Have you ever dealt with any of these? Explain? What did you do to get free from these attacks?

_____
_____
_____
_____
_____

7. In the lesson, "The Prophet and Emotionalism," what did we learn that the prophet do when under emotional attack?

_____
_____
_____
_____
_____
_____
_____
_____

We hope that you have learned something from this lesson

*This is the end of this section. *

The Prophet and Holiness

"Make every effort to live in peace with everyone and to be holy; without holiness no one will see the Lord." - Hebrews 12:14 (NIV)

" Holiness is a lifestyle that births a movement. "- Ashley Reynolds

1. In the lesson, "The Prophet and Holiness," We learned that holy living should be at the _____ of the budding prophets desire.

2. According to the Lesson, "The Prophet and Holiness," What is the reason why we cannot see the error of our ways?_____
_____
_____
_____
_____

3. In the lesson, "The Prophet and Holiness," we learned that you can operate in your prophetic gift but if not holy you can die and go to _____

4. This is because of what Romans 11:29 (WEB) says, " For the _____ and the _____of God are _____." This Scripture reveals that one can operate in the gift of prophecy without being holy.

5. Leviticus 19:2 (NKJV), "be ye _____ for _____ the _____ your God am _____."

6. Do you think that it is enough to solely depend on your gift? Yes or No. Please explain your answer._____
_____
_____
_____
_____

80

7. In the lesson, "The Prophet and Holiness," we learned that holiness is not a _____ but it is a _____

8. According to the Lesson, "The Prophet and Holiness," we learned that holiness is not tied to several things. Name a few of those things:

    1. _____

    2. _____

    3. _____

9. Do you agree with these?

_____

_____

_____

_____

_____

We hope that you have learned something from this lesson

*This is the end of this section. *

The Prophet and Sexual Perversion

"But the cowardly, the unbelieving, the vile, the murderers, the sexually immoral, those who practice magic arts, the idolaters and all liars--they will be consigned to the fiery lake of burning sulfur. This is the second death." - Revelation 21:8 (NIV)

"Sex outside of marriage or expressed perversely is not worth your soul damnation. God can keep you. Let him do so! "- Ashley Reynolds

1. According to the lesson, "The Prophet and Sexual Perversion," there was some terminology defined surrounding sexuality. Please define these:

1. Perversion   -

   _____

   _____

   _____

2. Homosexuality-

   _____

   _____

   _____

3. Bi-sexuality-

   _____

   _____

   _____

4. Hetero-sexual-

   _____

_____

_____

5. Abomination   -

_____

_____

_____

6. Desolation-

_____

_____

_____

2. According to the lesson, "The Prophet and Sexual Perversion," Homosexuality is a major attack on Gods prophets. Why is this so?

_____

_____

_____

_____

3. Romans 1:26-27 (NKJV) states:

"For this reason _____ gave them over to _____ passions; for their women _____ the _____ function for that which is _____, and in the same way also the men _____ the _____ function of the woman and burned in their desire toward one another, _____ with

_____ committing _____ acts and receiving in their own persons the due penalty of their _____. These verses shows us how that homosexuality is an abomination which leads to desolation."

4. What does the word speak about beastality? Deuteronomy 27:21 (NKJV):

"_____ is he who _____ with any _____.' And all the people shall say, 'Amen.'

5. In the lesson, "The Prophet and Sexual Perversion," We learned that the prophet can operate under 2 types of spirits. What are they?:

1. _____

_____

2. _____

_____

6. Which ones are pure and which ones are impure?

_____

_____

_____

_____

7. What does it mean to be tempted and what does it mean to be tainted?

_____

_____

84

_____

_____

8. Do you believe that the prophet of God can be delivered from any sexual bondage? If so, How?

_____

_____

_____

_____

_____

9. According to Revelation 21:8 (NIV) what will happen to those who practice sexual immorality?

_____

_____

_____

_____

10. Do you struggle with sexual perversion? I would advise you to seek Godly counsel while seeking the Lord for deliverance. There is strength in numbers.

We hope that you have learned something from this lesson

*This is the end of this section. *

Lying Prophets vs. False Prophets

Is there a Difference?

"Beware of false prophets, who come to you in sheep's clothing but inwardly are ravenous wolves."- Matthew 7:15 (ESV)

"The old prophet answered, "I too am a prophet, as you are. And an angel said to me by the word of the LORD: 'Bring him back with you to your house so that he may eat bread and drink water." (But he was lying to him.)- 1 Kings 13:18 (NIV)

"It is possible to be a true prophet that lie. It is impossible to be a false prophet and represent truth. Try the spirit by the spirit."- Ashley Reynolds

1. Using your dictionary, define these terminologies:

    1. False:

    _____

    _____

    2. Liar:

    _____

    _____

2. According to Matthew 24:24 (KJV), what two false people will rise up in the last days?

    1. False _____

    2. False _____

3. According to Matthew 24:24, these false people will rise up and perform what 2 acts?

    1. _____

    2. _____

4. According to Matthew 24:24, what will be the agenda of these 2 false ministries?_____

_____

5. According to the lesson, "Lying Prophets vs. False Prophets; Is there a Difference?," we learned that lying prophets lie with their _____ while false prophets lie with their whole_____.

6. In the lesson, "Lying Prophets vs. False Prophets; Is there a Difference?," we learned that lying prophets can still be _____ prophets of God while false prophets are people who have _____ been _____ by God to be his prophet.

7. In the lesson, "Lying Prophets vs. False Prophets; Is there a Difference?," we learned of some typical traits of lying prophets. Name 3:

      1.

      2.

      3.

8. In the lesson, "Lying Prophets vs. False Prophets; Is there a Difference?," we learned some traits of false prophets. Name 3:

      1.

      2.

      3.

9. After reading my testimony of the "Hillary Clinton" dream, do you think this was a sign of a lying (wrong interpretation) prophet or a false prophet? Explain your answer.

_____

_____

_____

_____

_____

We hope that you have learned something from this lesson

*This is the end of this section. *

Prophetic Authorities

"Behold, I have given you authority..."- Luke 10:19 (ESV)

"With prophetic rank comes prophetic authority "- Ashley Reynolds

1. According to the lesson, "Prophetic Authorities," who gives the prophet his authority?

_____

2. Using your dictionary, define what authority means?_____

_____

_____

_____

3. Do you think that it is possible to have a successful and flourishing prophetic ministry without having authority?

_____

_____

_____

_____

4. According to the lesson, "Prophetic Authority," why do you think many prophets do not wait on the authority of God to move out in their prophetic ministries?

_____

_____

_____

_____

_____

_____

5. According to the lesson, "Prophetic Authority," do you agree that one of the reasons why prophets do not see having authority from God as a high quality because they have never valued authoritative figures? Explain your answer:

_____

_____

_____
_____
_____
_____
_____
_____
_____

6. In the lesson, "Prophetic Authority," we learned about 10 authorities that come with the prophetic mantle in due time. Name the top three authorities that you walk in or believe that God will one day grant you the liberty to walk in:

      1. _____

      2. _____

      3. _____

7. Why did you choose these three (3) authorities?

_____
_____
_____
_____
_____
_____
_____
_____

8. Has there ever been a time where you have ever disrespected an authority figure? If yes, explain why this happened?

_____
_____
_____
_____
_____
_____
_____

9. Are you healed from such experience?

_____

10. I encourage you to know that abuse of authority is at an all time high amongst the prophetic arena. However, you don't have to join in with them. Whenever you are mistreated by other authority figures do not retaliate from your flesh. I encourage you to use your authority that was given you by the Lord to dismiss their folly. Pray for them, ask God to heal you from it and continue being a success in your ministry. It may take some time but God will make it possible. Selah

We hope that you have learned something from this lesson

*This is the end of this section. *

Prophetic Leadership

"He must become greater; I must become less." - John 3:30 (NIV)

" True leadership is not your opportunity to abuse people. Leadership is an open door for you to submit.
"- Ashley Reynolds

1. In the lesson, "Prophetic Leadership," we learned that when you are called to lead, God will give you height in the spirit. In doing this will the Lord make you distinguished from among those you lead.

Let's look at 1 Samuel 9:2 (b):   "from his _____ upward he was _____ than any of the people."

2. 1 Samuel 9:6 (NKJV) - "And he said to him, "Look now, there is in this city a _____ of _____, and he is an _____ man; _____ that he _____ surely comes to pass. So let us _____ there; perhaps _____ can _____ us the _____ that we should _____.""

   a. As a prophetic leader people will put trust in your leadership. The servant of Saul was able to testify to the credible prophetic leadership of Prophet Samuel.

3. James 4:10 (NIV)- "_____ yourselves before the Lord, and he will _____you up."

   a. This scripture shows how that elevation comes from God. When leaders submit under God they will find themselves walking in the high places.

4. So in _____, do to _____ what you would have them do to you, for this sums up the Law and the Prophets. - Matthew 7:12 (NIV)

   a. This scripture points to the fact that prophetic leadership is also about submitting righteous acts towards those that they interact with. When you are in prophetic leadership, it is never only about how good the people should treat the leader. Leadership is also about how good the leader should be treating the people. It is a partnership of upright behavior between both the leader and the people.

5. Philippians 2:3-4, (NIV) : "Do _____ out of _____ ambition or _____ conceit. Rather, in humility _____ others _____ yourselves, not looking to your own _____ but _____ of _____ to the interests of the _____."

    a. When in leadership, it's good to know that you are not leading people to use them for your own agenda. You are there to lead them in the way of the Lord and to avail yourself to serve them by helping to make dreams come true in their lives. Selah! (Pause. Think on this)

6. Proverbs 4:23, (NIV) - "_____ all else, _____ your _____, for everything you do _____ from it."

    a. This scripture shows how every leader should do a heart assessment. This will show you what kind of motives you have. This is important because it will help you to make sure that your motives are pure towards the people that you are leading and the things that you are doing for them.

7. Read 1 Samuel 9:13 (NKJV) - "As soon as you come into the city, you will surely find him before he goes up to the high place to eat. For the people will not eat until he comes, because he must bless the sacrifice; afterward those who are invited will eat. Now therefore, go up, for about this time you will find him."

    a. You will see how people will honor and respect you because they will realize the grace and blessing upon your life as a leader.

    b. Is there anything else that you see in this scripture?

_____

_____

_____

_____

_____

8. Young prophet as you grow more into your prophetic mantle, you will see how that you are chosen to lead in some capacity. Please know that while it is an honor to be chosen by God to lead his people, it is also a responsibility which calls for you to undergird such people in prayer and to lead and support them with much guidance from the Lord. I pray that you submit to God and allow him to help you carry the weight and responsibility of his people. You are chosen for this. Go forth!

We hope that you have learned something from this lesson

*This is the end of this section.

Prophetic Pain

"The LORD is close to the brokenhearted and saves those who are crushed in spirit." - Psalms 34:18 (NIV)

"Pain is a sign that you are carrying promise. Just before birthing comes pain. After pain comes relief. With relief victory."- Ashley Reynolds

1. Revelation 21:4 (NIV), "He will _____ every _____ from their eyes.." Years can be associated with pain.

2. 1 Peter 4:14 (NIV), "If you are _____ because of the name of Christ, you are _____, for the Spirit of _____ and of _____ rests on you.

3. In the lesson, "Prophetic Pain," we learned that Joseph's pain was not on account of his wrongdoing towards his brothers, but on account of him being _____ by his father and them knowing about it.

4. According to the lesson, "Prophetic Pain," do you think that carrying pain can stop you from fulfilling your God given assignment?

_____
_____
_____
_____

5. Can you think of a time when you felt pain? What happened?

_____
_____
_____
_____

6. How did you handle this pain? What did you do while experiencing this pain?

_____
_____

7. Young prophet, I encourage with this: "There is not pain that you can ever encounter that has the power to stop your destiny unless you give it to him. Jesus can heal you from every hurt. Choose your healing today."

We hope that you have learned something from this lesson

*This is the end of this section. *

Methodologies of God

"And he said, "Hear my words: If there is a prophet among you, I the LORD make myself known to him in a vision; I speak with him in a dream. Not so with my servant Moses. He is faithful in all my house. With him I speak mouth to mouth, clearly, and not in riddles, and he beholds the form of the LORD. Why then were you not afraid to speak against my servant Moses?" And the anger of the LORD was kindled against them, and he departed." - Numbers 12:6-8 (ESV)

"You learn differently; therefore God will speak to you accordingly!"- Ashley Reynolds

1. All prophets are different. This means that God deals with each of us according to our styles of learning.

2. In the Lesson, "Methodologies of God ," We learned several methods that God chooses to deal with his prophets. Name three (3) methods discussed and explain why you chose these three (3):

1. Method one:_____

   Reason for choosing this:

   _____
   _____
   _____
   _____
   _____

2. Method one:_____

   Reason for choosing this:

   _____
   _____
   _____
   _____
   _____

3. Method one:_____

   Reason for choosing this:

   _____
   _____
   _____
   _____
   _____

3. In the Lesson, "Methodologies of God ," what was so special with how the Lord chose to speak to the prophet Moses?

_____

_____

_____

_____

4. What is the definition of "vision"?

_____

_____

Give an example of who the Lord chose to communicate in this way:

_____

5. What is the definition of "dream"?

_____

_____

Give an example of who the Lord chose to communicate in this way:

_____

6. What is the definition of "element"?

_____

_____

Give an example of who the Lord chose to communicate in this way:

_____

7. How has the Lord been communicating to you lately?

_____

_____

_____

_____

8. Do you understand what the Lord is saying to you when he uses this method to communicate with you?

_____

9. Communication is key to any relationship. However, it is best that you know how you learn so that you can be more cognizant of when the Lord is speaking to you.

We hope that you have learned something from this lesson

*This is the end of this section. *

https://www.ashleyreynoldsministry.com/